# INTROVERT

A Practical Guide to Connecting With Others at
Networking Events and Beyond

(How to Leverage Your Unique Strengths to
Connect)

**Carmen Rand**

Published By Chris David

**Carmen Rand**

*Introvert: A Practical Guide to Connecting With Others at Networking Events and Beyond (How to Leverage Your Unique Strengths to Connect)*

ISBN 978-1-77485-276-7

Legal & Disclaimer

The information contained in this book is not designed to replace or take the place of any form of medicine or professional medical advice. The information in this book has been provided for educational and entertainment purposes only.

The information contained in this book has been compiled from sources deemed reliable, and it is accurate to the best of the Author's knowledge; however, the Author cannot guarantee its accuracy and validity and cannot be held liable for any errors or omissions. Changes are periodically made to this book. You must consult your doctor or get professional medical advice before using any of the suggested remedies, techniques, or information in this book.

Upon using the information contained in this book, you agree to hold harmless the Author from and against any damages, costs, and expenses, including any legal fees potentially resulting from the application of any of the information provided by this guide. This disclaimer applies to any damages or injury caused by the use and application, whether directly or indirectly, of any advice or information presented, whether for breach of contract, tort, negligence, personal injury, criminal intent, or under any other cause of action.

You agree to accept all risks of using the information presented inside this book. You need to consult a professional medical practitioner in order to ensure you are both able and healthy enough to participate in this program.

# TABLE OF CONTENTS

# Introduction

Studies have shown an average of 42% individuals are classified as introvert. Being an introvert isn't an easy task, but it's not difficult either. For those who are introverts it's easy to be seen as shy, quiet and not as "socially advanced" in comparison to your colleagues. Many prefer to be more extrovert to "fit with social norms" which makes them feel "in" instead of being seen as an outsider. What I've found out is that this is not true. I've come to realize that trying to alter the persona you're based on and changing your own unique personal characteristics isn't the best approach to succeed. Instead, it's essential to accept them and stay true to yourself.

If you're an introvert, you are the most perfect introvert there. You are not an extrovert. Whyis that? Doing your best to appear like you're not is likely to result in unnecessary anxiety, stress, and frustration because it's extremely difficult to alter character traits. However, it is important to note that you can always enhance their performance in social settings by with the help of emotional intelligence, and the willingness to leap into the fire and watch what happens.

The Introverted Leader concentrates on the inherent abilities that introverts possess instead of focusing on the things they aren't able to do.

There's nothing wrong with being insecure, you just value the quiet and time for yourself, both of which are wonderful attributes. Consider how wonderful you feel to be among the people who are content or even content by you. For those who are introverts you're likely to prefer connecting to one-on-one instead of interacting with a crowd of people.

Through this book, you'll be taught methods to make the most value from networking and business events to make it easier for both you and your company to flourish!

# Chapter 1: The Well-Known Introverts

Through the time of history the most revolutionary leaders as well as mathematicians, writers and inspiring messengers have walked the same ground that you're on and been recognized for their achievements not due to fame, but rather because of an unending desire to serve the world.

You can be a captivating introvert. It is crucial to keep in mind that you are not the only one. A third of individuals are considered introverts. The person who is sitting in front of you right now might be an introvert.

Although some research suggests that extroverted people are more ideal as leaders because of their innate confidence and unparalleled social skills, history has witnessed that some of the most glorified and influential leaders are actually soft-spoken, timid, and philosophically-minded introverts.

Abraham Lincoln (1809-1865)

Many people recognize his name as the tall man who sits upon the Memorial located in Washington, D.C. Others think of him as the person who was featured on that $5 note. A quick review of his background will reveal that it was the 16th President of the United States of America from 1861 until his assassination 1865. The most notable achievements of his presidency included his Gettysburg Address and the abolition of slavery in the U.S. with the passing of the 13th amendment.Many people are unaware that he wasn't the intimidating or striking force that media outlets have created him to be.

The historians have introduced Honest Abe back to world as a quiet, shy man. He was aware of the implications of abolishing slavery in the era of and was aware that the issue was not likely to be enacted in the usual method.

Long hours of reflection sometimes got into some way with his relationships with others and his focus on his family. It was apparent in his interactions to his child. Additionally, historians often assert the following: Abraham Lincoln was a man who was not one to offend anyone by his power.

Barack Hussein Obama II (Born: August 4, 1961- )

Apart from his being the very first African American president to ever serve within the U.S., President Obama is an introvert.

People who are introverts believe that their energy is well-used when they are engaged in solitude-based activities like writing or reading, as well as thinking. The president Obama wrote a variety of books. One of them is his memoir, Dreams from My Father. In the book, he wrote, "In my solitude I feel most secure." The book he wrote before that, The Audacity of Hope told the first few years of his affair with his first woman, Michelle. He described how he would frequently spend the evening, hunkered down in his office at the rear of his railroad apartment and pondering this as normal, while making his bride feel abandoned and lonely.

Albert Einstein (1879-1955)

You've heard it a thousand times and seen it many times in numerous resources from the classroom to pop culture. Albert Einstein's relativity theory has been around for a long time. All introverts will be at ease, as Einstein is one of the greatest minds of the past humanity is an eminent introvert.

Some might argue that Einstein is far from an introvert , due to his constant "conquest" of women companions and say Einstein would have accomplished much more had it not for these dazzling relationships and the constant excursions.

However, the truth is that Albert Einstein was an introvert. There's a possibility that If you're an introvert and reading this article and you like one of his assertions: "When I examine myself and my thinking processes I arrive at an understanding that my ability of fantasy has been more meaningful for me than any ability for abstract optimistic thinking." Perhaps that is more specific: "The monotony and solitude of a life that is quiet can stimulate the mind to think creatively."

William Henry Gates III (Born on October 28, 1955 - )

If you're not living under the surface you're likely to find that you've heard who this person is. He was named the world's richest person from 1995 to 2009 and was able to claim the title again in 2013.

If your birthdate falls at the period of the explosion technological revolution, then you probably have utilized the software or program that Bill Gates is most well-known for. William Henry Gates III, or more commonly "Bill" Gates is the co-founder and former chairman and chief executive officer of Microsoft. He left his position as chairperson of Microsoft in February. 2014 and took the role as a technology advisor for the newly named Chief Executive Officer, Satya Nadella.

Gates is involved in numerous charitable activities. Through this, the foundation has contributed a substantial amount of money to various charity organizations, aid organizations as well as scientific research funding via his foundation, the Bill and Melinda Gates Foundation.

A writer on The Psychology Today blog once wrote that "Bill Gates is quiet and literary, however, he seems unfazed by other opinion of him."

Stephen Gary Wozniak (Born: August 11, 1950 - )

Steve"The Woz," or "The Woz" is the co-founder of Apple Computers and the developer of the Apple II computer. In the early days, International Business Machines (IBM) was a major player in the creation in personal computer technology. With his outstanding technical and programming abilities along with Jobs's marketing effectiveness The Woz was able propel Apple to the level of success it has today.

Steve Jobs as well as Steve Jobs single-handedly built the very first computers that were the basis for the revolution of microcomputers.

It is believed it is believed that Steve Wozniak is a known introvert who would remain at home during office hours to create ideas on his own in his cubicle as he believed it was more easy to think about ideas with everyone else in the office gone.

Joanne Jo Rowling (Born: July 31, 1965 - pen names are: J.K. Rowling and Robert Galbraith)

They are not only scientists or innovators. They can also be creative. The most well-known writers of the last decade has acknowledged that she is an introvert. It is J.K. Rowling, the creator of the bestseller Harry Potter series and the critically acclaimed films that came after, J.K. Rowling.

The idea for the Harry Potter character Harry Potter came to Rowling as she was travelling on her own in the 1990s. Interviews with her talked about her excitement at the time and how strongly she felt about that particular concept and the inspiration. She went on to say that she didn't have any papers at the time and the pen she was carrying wasn't working at all. However she was hesitant about borrowing a pen from one of her friends. The wait was on for an unreliable train for 4 hours to go to Manchester to London and was sitting in the waiting room with all her ideas putting them together in her mind. In the end, she wrote: "...this unassuming, black-haired bespectacled, black-haired boy who had no idea that he was a wizard grew ever more tangible for me."

The publishers of the time believed that the concept behind the book was a bit far-fetched. The book was rejected by 12 different publishing houses in England. However, after a few years and a half, the book finally got the light at beginning of the tunnel when it was given the green signal from Bloomsbury, the publisher. Bloomsbury located in London. Presently it is believed that the Harry Potter brand is now an international brand worth $15 billion.

As you might have already guessed the importance of solitude, it is a key aspect of true creativity. Writers usually sit working at their computers and typewriters or pen and paper as they come up with their thoughts. Sometimes, it's groundbreaking work such as J.K. Rowling's. It's no doubt for those who are introverts and find pleasure in isolation, sooner or later the continuous flow of inspiration and constant determination to discover the perfect way to think will yield the next great idea.

# Chapter 2: How Do You Strengthen Yourself as an introvert?

If you ask most introverts, they'll share times when they felt unusual due to their inherent desire for solitude. This chapter will discuss the advantages of introverts and because introverts are often thought to be shy and quiet and shy, we'll begin with a trait that may seem a bit confusing initially.

Excellent conversationalists!

Although it may seem, introverts are, indeed excellent conversators. In addition to the fact of being in tune with the subject matter They are also excellent listeners. What is an exchange without listening? Their appearance may appear like that however, most introverts have a tendency for listening, paying close attentively and take a deep breath before speaking. It is evident that introverts do not actively engage in conversations with people who they're not very familiar with. But they're adept at maintaining and having good conversations with people who they are able to connect with, such as close family members, friends and even mentors. Being an introvert your dislike for small talk and the public attention shouldn't place you in the middle of the pack. Your need for profound and relevant conversations is valid, however, you don't know where to discover this, so it's fine to allow people to have a go. It's okay to some small chats occasionally. Sometimes, this kind of conversation could lead to deeper conversations.

Watching

The introverts have the ability to focus much more than those who have other personalities. Why is this? Because introverts learn through the process of observation. It's good news that when these skills can be applied to the academic and business fields, success is never distant! If you're an introvert consider the instances when you saw things others did not immediately notice. The ability to concentrate and be more critical is certainly a boon and when it is directed towards your job, relationship as well as education could be very useful.

Creativity

Solitude is the best place to develop creativity and no one loves solitude more than introverts do. Writing is an instinctual trait of introverts. A lot of introverts think twice about how to express their thoughts verbally and so prefer creating writing for self-expression. Writing however, isn't the only arena that introverts flourish. There are introverts who excel in all areas, such as computer programming, acting and even computer gaming.

Prioritizing

This is a characteristic and strength of the introverted persona that allows them to be efficient employees. Due to this characteristic introverts are capable of maintaining the ability to have a balance between work and personal life. People who are introverted are self-motivated and accomplish their tasks without being controlled. They aren't a fan of being micro-managed.

Team Players

It's quite surprising, isn't it? Individuals who prefer autonomy are more successful when it comes to their work but they are able to be teammates. To work as a team, there has to be collaboration and unity. When everyone is fighting to be heard and seen but the introverts aren't. Unity and peace are much more crucial to those who prefer to not be heard. But that doesn't mean they are little to offer to the community. People who are introverts are often not full of ideas.

Unique Leadership Skills

Although introverts aren't typically considered to be leaders but they do, in reality make excellent leaders. Leadership goes beyond an enthralling voice, a charming smile, and an unwavering handshake. People who are introverts have the ability to create profound, meaningful relationships. they are sensitive to emotional signals and can detect signals that may not be communicated. This is crucial when there is a shared objective to be met. In addition, since they do not look for their own spotlights, they provide their colleagues the chance for them to be noticed and felt appreciated.

Overthinking

This could be viewed as an advantage, and it could be. However, the fact is that introverts are able to go through events repeatedly in their minds is also a benefit. What's the reason? Because, through overthinking introverts are able to spot potential issues. This is a huge advantage in the workplace. If the introvert isn't letting their overthinking stop them from doing the things they need to do and executing their actions, thinking too much could be a benefit.

Good Listeners

This is a great benefit for introverts in the workplace at school, or in leadership positions. Listening is an essential aspect of communicating. If this skill is utilized effectively, introverts will be successful in nearly every area of their lives.

## Chapter 3: The Best Listener & Observer

Although extroverts naturally leap at the first opportunity to be the main attraction on the stage, introverts gifted with the rare ability of focus, reassurance and fine detail. These are amazing tools that allow us to to tap into the energy reservoir for improving all aspects which we engage in. Being attentive can be an benefit at work, home at school, or even during games. We'd like to explore further in the subject...

We're looking for ways we can increase the natural abilities that we are born with. That's why...

Don't run--listen

You can't be at home every day. Therefore, when you're not in your favourite spot or when you feel like you feel exhausted in more energetic situations, don't quit. Sometimes, you have the chance to do something no one else in the room is doing or can't be better than you - listen. You are able to open your senses by absorbing the energy that you've brought from your corner and take into a new perspective.

Even if you don't have a preference for social gatherings and parties and gatherings, your growing knowledge will be able to assist you ease your displeasure for these events and assist you to adapt and adjust better than you it was possible! At the end of the day you'll still be what you are, you will be much more educated just because you were attentive...

Sit down and observe

Listening isn't the only way to be better. Observation is also visual and the less distracted person would naturally be the best observer. People who are introverts are more observant. It is possible to squirm, and there are times when you'll be counting down the minutes to get home to recharge your batteries, but be sure to remember that being at work is to your advantage. Anywhere you go take advantage of the chance to perform better when you're low.

If you're a parent, you'll notice that you have a better grasp of the way things work even with kids in comparison to your extrovert companion because you're more attentive and aware. If one of your kids decides to adopt a new habit that they don't like, you'll be the first one to notice. Also, if your children or even your spouse is rumbling away with excitement, you'll be the perfect listener. However, extroverts are inclined to talk about themselves... They do not like listening. They want to be the driver, talk more and listen less. At the end of the day you'll be a unifying families and it will be due to the power that you have derived from your simple introverted nature.

When you work, you'll discover that you have a greater understanding of the way things function than the majority of people due to the fact that you've been more attentive and aware. Although modern workplaces are packed with people and ambiances, you'll find the introvert within you establishing a niche that combines the highest level of competence and a shrewd personality, which is attributed to your increased awareness of the environment you work in. When we examine the tips for working in the next chapter, you'll see how crucial these characteristics are for the introvert on the process of pursuing a job or working in chaos in the workplace.

In school, you will be amazed at how easily you fit into a group. You're more likely be able to understand the others and are able to cope with them all. The majority of them are trying to assert their leadership positions and such. Your listening and observational ability allow you to tap the most difficult tool that students require-- patience. It is patience for team members as well as perseverance for instructors, and patience for every aspect... They are constantly moving and there is no time to listen, which means there is there is no time to record the most important information. Introverts can quickly rise up the academic ladder, but he can easily fall back into his typical introvert traits , and then incorporating these traits into a larger life that is purposeful.

How can we improve our ability to pay attention?

Are you aware of the meaning of meditation? It's a good thing, because whether you like it or not, it's the best method to improve your focus and become more attentive at the smallest details. Meditation helps you resist any major or minor thing that are happening around you, and free your mind of any distractions. When you are in this state, it is possible to prepare yourself to concentrate on a single aspect whenever you choose to.

Another option is to focus on only one thing at a. This means that you should not take on multiple tasks and expect to remain focus. For an introvert like you it can be very harmful. You'll get exhausted or angry quickly and you'll be tempted to quit and go to your own 'alone space to relax. When you're improving your focus and abilities, do the exercise in small increments to to fully benefit from the workout.

However sharp your brain iseven if you manage to concentrate on a crying baby at the top of the noisy football field, you must be aware of the degree of distraction that surrounds you is not too complex and overwhelming for you. Start small. Don't practice in difficult scenarios; choose areas that have less distractions. So, focusing becomes more easy to achieve and you're less likely to feel exhausted in a short time.

Oh I'm sorry, but do you know what? Take care to eat right! Yes, eat right and eat at the right time. Your health is crucial to the success of whatever you set out to accomplish and anything that is involving your brain requires that your body be well-prepared. Make sure you're eating healthy and are not overeating yourself for fear of being uncomfortable with others. Keep in mind that you should be refueled before heading out for any "extro" tasks. We've all heard that being outside of the "zone is exposing us to the draining of our energy.

When you are utilizing the art of keeping an eye on an effective strategy, remember to take the appropriate precautions and remain fit to get the most effective results.

## Chapter 4: Strategies for an introvert. How to Survive Social Gatherings.

Although introverts like to be alone and prefer not be at social gatherings, there comes a point when they have to step out of their comfort zone to mix with other people. Here are some guidelines that can aid those who are the least introverted person to feel at ease with other people.

Let's first look at scenarios and events that could be prevented. There are also situations that can't be avoided. Sounds simple right? But the problem is that introverts find a reason to stay away from all occasions and do not realize there are occasions when their presence is necessary.

Things which you should (optionally) stay clear of.

* Meetups every week. Certain groups of people consider an occasional catch-up at the local coffee shop or bar as an absolute requirement. Television shows that are popular are typically inspired by these kinds of establishments (think Cheers, Friends and How I Met Your Mother) however, you don't have to be present at every gathering.

* Weddings of people who you don't know: When people who are people who are extroverts receive invitations for any social event they see it as an opportunity to connect with new people. For an introvert, it's appropriate to decline invitations to your former roommate's brother's wedding!

* Going out to places for purposes of dating The appeal of dating websites online is that you can meet new people in your home and not have to leave. This

does not mean that there is something wrong with traditional ways of meeting however introverts have found an innovative method of meeting potential partners.

You should not avoid certain situations.

• Networking opportunities: You risk not making growth in your career if do not attend every gathering. Select your events with care and ensure there are attendees you can trust.

* Special events for close family and friends The point is that no matter how much you would like to stay in your home, it is crucial to spend Christmas with your family or your closest friends. Birthdays and weddings must also be celebrated with family and friends. Sometimes, they may not take your introverted lifestyle as a reason to excuse yourself.

* Your own personal events If you feel like the last thing you'd like to do is create the most of your birthday or work-related promotion. It's not that difficult to recognize that it's not about you! Your family and friends would like to join in your celebrations and are entitled to share the celebration. The good thing is that you have some control over the size of your gathering and the contents. Rememberthat people are only looking to share their experiences to you out of love.

If you must go to an event Here are some suggestions to help you get through the event.

• Bring two conversation starters as well as an intriguing story.

The most common conversations that can allow you to connect with others include holidays, pets, travel and sports, recipes, as well as food and activities. The topics you will see can help people talk and relieve pressure from you.

Always have an interesting story to tell in your arsenal of conversation. It should be something interesting, funny concise, and inclusive. Make sure you know the details of you're going to be drinking before the event!

* Wear a topic for conversation

If you own a funny tie or a unique item of jewelry, it is possible to get people talking when they inquire about the item. Provide them with an incentive to talk to you and then extend the conversation.

* Make use of your extrovert friends

Tagging a friend that can make conversations easily will help you gain access to a social setting. Let your friend begin the conversation, later, sneak in and provide your thoughts.

• Find work accomplish

When an introvert is in an area that is crowded, all that they will see is space packed with people talking and having fun. They think that no one cares about their thoughts and they feel totally alone. We are aware that this isn't an accurate perception of the situation, but how are you doing to be less powerless?

If you spot empty glasses or plates, pick them up and go for your kitchen. If you see an empty plate of food sitting on a table, pick it up and go for large groups of people. Food can be an excellent way to break the ice and you'll feel like you're doing something. After a few minutes, you'll feel more at ease because you have a job to fill.

* Power pose

Your posture will help you feel more comfortable. Stand with your legs separated and your hands on your the hips for two minutes and you will feel confident. Imagine "superhero posture" and let your confidence rise.

* Take a look at the details of a retreat

There are times when you feel your energy levels have dropped prior to the party is over and you're in need of some "me time". If you are at an event, look for an opening for bolts and utilize it when it is needed. It could be a garden or bathroom, or kitchen, or even your vehicle. A few minutes away the noise can give you an important relief from the external noise and help you take your breath.

* Make sure to book your event for peaceful times

When you can, try to spend time prior to an important event by engaging in things that relax your soul. You can read a book, watch an Netflix movie marathon or simply sit down. Do whatever keeps you relaxed. The energy you put into your brain will assist you in dealing with the energy and noise of the day ahead.

It is important to allow some time to unwind after the party. You will not only have some space for your self after a long night, but you'll also have something you can anticipate.

* Make sure you have an escape plan

As an introvert, it is important that you must be aware of what you can do when an event is too excessive for you. If you rely on a transportation service to home, you'll be feeling more stress throughout the occasion. It is important to have your own transportation or an alternative that is reliable.

Also, you should not be someone else's driver since this could put limits on the time you can leave. Being in control can help you feel comfortable with unfamiliar surroundings and the company.

The most important thing to remember is to remember that the people you meet are curious about you and would love to get to know you! Your mind may tell that people do not have any interest in you and aren't at all interested in you, but this is a flimsy assumption! Get out and make new friends and it is definitely worth it.

## Chapter 5: The Art of Putting Yourself out There

You must go out. You'll need acquaintances and make new acquaintances. If you are confined to your own space for longer than you should, it will be a sign to your brain that socializing with other people is a challenging task, which only people who are social are able to do.

This will make you more afraid of people. Also, you'll lose the chance to improve your social abilities. While you may not be naturally outgoing You must rise for the moment and engage in socializing whenever the mood calls for it.

Take a Commitment

Socializing is about making the decision to begin hanging out more. You must make the decision. This will increase your social horizons open so that you can take advantage of every opportunity to having a conversation with people.

The majority of people are aware of that piece of information. Yet, many people choose to overlook it. Perhaps it's because they are lazy or simply the inability to face reality, they hinder their chances of making more friends.

How can you make the possibility of interfacing just a bit more?

Start by setting goals, and they must be SMART for it to be successful. The acronym states that goals should be:

Specific - clearly define the goal you are trying to accomplish. Would you like to establish an alliance of people who could help you land an opportunity to work? Are you looking to find the person you've always wanted to be with?

Measurable - You must be able measure your progress towards your goals. You could tell yourself, "I will talk to 1 person a day." You could also declare, "I will be going to a gathering once every two weeks."

It is possible - we all know that introverts don't like being in large groups of people. Therefore, while being around 20 strangers on a daily basis is possible, for most introverts, it's not healthy. This goal will not be a good one.

Relevant - The goal should be pertinent to your current situation. If you're trying to create an alliance of people who can assist you with your career by focusing on relationships with those who are not employed in and of themselves is not going to assist.

Timing is everything. Deadlines are crucial. They force us off our feet and force us to reach our objectives. So, your objective should have a date that must be accomplished. This should be realistic, however it shouldn't be too relaxed.

After you've set your idea, you can write it down on the paper and put it at your desk or wherever you can easily see it. A desk can be an excellent example. So you won't need to remind yourself that you've got the obligation of meeting.

Studies have shown that writing things down improves the chances of being successful. Writing down your ideas will be your first move to changing a desire into realisation.

Here are some additional tips to improve your chances of reaching your final goal:

Start small - when beginning something new, many of us are eager to accomplish as much as we can in as little time as is possible. Therefore, we set plans that are often too ambitious. Although you might be able to make a lot of new acquaintances at first however, it will be difficult to maintain over the long term. You will feel the entire process stressful. It is important to begin with a small amount. You could, for example, aim to make contact with just one person each week. It's a simple goal to not quit.

Monitor your progress. Many we tend to believe that once we have set an objective, there is nothing that could go wrong. However, this isn't reality. Goals do not always go as planned. The future is always unpredictable and you cannot anticipate it.

If you have said that you will go out more often do you go out as you had planned? A question like this will help ensure that you're adhering to your plan. Otherwise, you may abandon the plan and not realizing what you've accomplished. It is possible to track your goal each day, every week or even once a month. The nature of your objective will determine.

Inform others about your plans Your family and friends are likely to be delighted to see you achieve your goals that you've set. Telling them should be among your main goals. They won't just encourage you, but they will be your teachers and mentors, but you will also be responsible to them. If you ever feel like not achieving your goals, you'll be thinking about it twice. No one likes to make mistakes particularly in the eyes of those who matter to him.

Place yourself in social situations

When we think about putting yourself in social situations, the majority of you can easily imagine going to bars or to parties often. Although these can be helpful however, they're not the only methods. In reality, for other introverts, these strategies may not be the best option.

There are plenty of ways to connect with others without having go beyond your comfortable zone.

One of the most effective methods is to engage in something you enjoy with others. If you want reading a novel, to the park or sit in a café. It is likely that you will become bored of your book. This is the perfect time to begin an exchange with someone close to you.

If you're always taking lunch to work, consider eating in an eatery. There are many people who are new to you that you can meet.

Instead of exercising outside in the backyard consider exercising in the gym or at the park. In reality, many people are uncomfortable working out on their own. You may end up having as a fitness buddy.

How to make yourself likable and approachable

Going to parties or the park doesn't guarantee you'll get to meet someone. Your conduct when out and about matters a huge lot. It is important to attract people attracted to your character. You must attract their interest. You must appear friendly so that they aren't scared to take a look at them.

You may have seen the situation at a gathering that some guests aren't addressed by anyone. It could be that they haven't made themselves available to be approached.

Being approachable doesn't need you to do anything untoward. (No necessity to

shout, or stand in tables to be recognized.)
Here are some of my suggestions:

Smile . A simple smile can be a blessing for you. It lets you know that you're satisfied. Happiness is like an illness that spreads to everyone in your vicinity. Additionally, a cheerful appearance is interesting, pleasant and attractive.

This doesn't mean that you must make a huge grin. You'll make others who are around you, and they will not be able to approach you. If someone is looking at you make sure you give them a genuine smile. That means you need to look at your eyes too and not just your lips. Take a look in an mirror. Imagine a funny story . See the way you smile. Try to fake a smile. Do you notice a difference? It is important to do the first.

Do not be distracted - you can do this in various ways, starting with being consumed with your surroundings or even your thoughts. If you're in an eatery and you're preoccupied with your laptop or phone the people around you will think that they will be interrupted by your thoughts. And they'll be careful not to disturb them.

If you're able to create an expression that suggests your mind is wandering Mars Again, people won't be able to approach you.

Instead, take everything out and be in the moment. Take a look around and take an active curiosity about the people who are around you. Be relaxed.

Pay attention to your posture. This is another tool we can employ to attract people to our side. The position of standing with your arms crossed in front is an defensive posture. The people who are in this position will not be able to steer clear of your position. If you're sitting or standing, you should ensure that you're standing straight. Your arms should extend to your sides.

Create Eye Contact - this clearly indicates that you are attracted to an individual. It also allows them to make contact with you. You may also get permission to talk to them. If you are looking at someone, it is important to keep your conversation short. It is also helpful to add a smile.

Mirror the other Person People like to mirror those that look similar to them. This is why you can utilize this psychological technique in your favor. To demonstrate this, we'll look at a study conducted that was conducted by Theodore Newcomb. Participants were asked to share their views on topics related to politics and religion. They were later put in a single room. It was interesting to note that people were drawn to people with similar attitudes.

Therefore, try to show how you're like your counterpart in whatever way that you could. In a subtle way, try to emulate what they're doing. If you try to mirror too much you will end up doing the opposite. If someone else is using hands to communicate Try talking by using your hands. If they're still and quiet, try the same.

Develop confidence

Confidence is a wonderful trait to exhibit in social situations. Not only will others find them attractive but also it also helps make you feel comfortable. Instead of feeling nervous you'll enjoy the conversation. Instead of feeling tired you will feel rejuvenated.

Concentrate on Your Strengths

Sometimes, we tend to concentrate on what that we're not able to do. We criticize ourselves believing that we aren't sufficient because we have weak points in certain areas. This can only decrease confidence in ourselves.

Instead, focus on your strengths and utilize these strengths to increase your confidence. There is no need to be a pro in all things. You are probably already proficient in just one or two things. That's what makes you special. It also will give you a an opportunity to share your story with others and encourage them to do the same.

It is possible that you don't like being with strangers, however, you might have a great personality. It is possible that you don't like being around many persons, yet you might be a fantastic storyteller, or have the basics of many things, which gives you an endless array of topics to keep the conversation going.

When you concentrate on all of these strengths, you'll discover that you're not worthless. You do not require the approval from others to realize that you are unique. You are your own greatest admirer.

Make Sure You Look Your Best

Unattractive appearance is one of the reasons why you should be avoiding people. Try to dress well before going out. Maintain a good hygiene routine and maintain your wardrobe. There is no need to spend money on trendy clothes or expensive items. It is possible to wear basic and affordable clothes. There's a wealth of tips online about how to dress well. Use this advice to benefit.

Try to appear confident

While this might sound strange it is true that acting confidently can be a good way to feel more confident. The reason for this isn't entirely evident however, it happens. It could be due in the sense that our brains is unable to distinguish between imagination and reality. The mind is a game.

If you aren't sure how to create confidence consider people you know who are confident. It could be a acquaintance, a family member or even a film actor. You can adopt their character and do your best to conform to it.

# Chapter 6: Coping with Your Social Beliefs

Do you feel anxious about being in a crowd of people? Do you get worried when you're planning meeting new friends?

Understanding the Issue

If that's the case, you must to know the reason. It is also important to determine the elements that are associated with being in crowds or meeting new people that cause you to be nervous. There is a common pattern in the way anxiety or fear grows. In the majority of cases, it begins with an event that triggers. The fear could begin when you are told that you must attend the social gatherings. Certain introverts simply do not like social gatherings when they did not anticipate it. They may be afraid when they have to participate in an activity that draws their attention on them. The fear usually is due to their performance in a social context.

It is normal to be scared. It's a natural method for our bodies to alert that we are in danger. But, it can also be debilitating socially, especially when fear becomes a way of keeping us from fulfilling our job.

Take Mike for an example. Mike is about to celebrate his third Christmas with the company. He hasn't been to the two initial Christmas celebrations of the company as there are always events that make him feel embarrased. He tries to persuade himself into attending the event but the fear of being embarrassed always wins. Over the last 2 years, he usually chooses, at the spur of the moment to stay at home and come up with an excuse to explain why he cannot be there.

The last two holidays celebrations, Mike did not understand the reason he doesn't wish to attend. But, when he looked at the patterns of his anxiety, he realized it was the way he was acting in the crowd which made him nervous. He loved the idea of enjoying a great time with his coworkers and enjoys having conversations with some of them. However, whenever the thought of doing something in front of his colleagues pops into his head and he starts to feel nervous. He begins to imagine scenarios in which it is difficult to perform.

If he knows the exact part of the event that Mike is afraid of, he might be able to steer clear of the part that involves performing instead of having to miss the entire occasion completely.

Triggers are the thoughts about social events that trigger the anxiety in your brain. Once the fear begins an individual who is socially anxious is prone to a series of behaviors that cause the person to avoid social occasions. In the workplace being absent from certain events or events could be considered as not being an active participant in the team.

To stop your social phobia hindering your from doing what you want to do, you must to determine the exact cause of your anxiety. Here are a few most common social events that people avoid:

* Public speaking

Doing something when an enormous crowd is watching

The feeling of being teased or laughing at

* Presenting before those with authority

* Going out on a date, or having a meeting with someone you're interested in

* Performing on stage

* Beginning an informal conversation

Most people recognize that the things they are afraid of the most aren't really important and they are able to overcome it. But, some introverts fail to get the strength to face their fears, even when they realize that the situation they fear might not occur. Here are a few ways you can take to stop your fear from overtaking your actions:

Control the way you think to face your fears

There are certain thought patterns that people who are anxious in social situations often utilize. Here are some:

* Assumptions, predictions and assumptions

People who are worried believe that there will always be a chance to be embarrassed in any event for them to feel embarrassed. They make many assumptions that result in their anxiety. They also make forecasts on the way things will unfold. For those who suffer from social anxiety it becomes a routine.

If you start thinking and anticipating frightening scenarios this is a sign that you must distract your mind from the anxiety. There are different ways to cope to deal with anxiety. If you're in the office and the anxiety strikes for instance, you may distract yourself with tasks to stop it from dominating your thoughts.

* Extremely negative thoughts

The theories and beliefs of introverts with social anxiety are often exacerbated by their extreme negative attitude. When they think of these things they think of the worst that can occur.

* Personalizing

When they think of possibilities of things going wrong at social gatherings the party goers also consider how people at the gathering will react to them. They believe that the people in the party want to laugh at them. They think that their bosses are out to humiliate them.

* The fight or flight response

If the fear is triggered the stress hormones trigger their fight or flight response. For introverts with social anxiety the first reaction is to steer clear of the situation. They might have made the decision to go to the occasion in the past, but they were able to make it work. When they were faced with similar stress they chose to employ similar responses to the stress.

As time passes the patterns of thinking become automatic when forced to attend an event they don't know about. The continued use of these patterns of behavior and thinking prevents individuals from enjoying the benefits of the social benefits.

How can you prevent social Fears?

Exercises to breathe

Breathing is among the very few tasks that the body can perform with both the subconscious and conscious mind. Being capable of controlling the unconscious actions of breathing through being aware of them is a potent instrument. One of the initial signs of anxiety is an increase in the rate of breathing in shallow breaths. It can happen as you prepare to leave for the event. It could also happen when you are thinking about the occasion. When you experience this it is best to get back control over your breathing. If, for instance, you notice that you're feeling anxious or nervous about a particular social event then you must sit in your seat and practice the following breathing exercises:

1. Relax on your chair with you back upright and head towards the front. Place the right side of your hand onto the lap of your right and your left rests on the top of your stomach.

2. Take a slow, deep breath through your nose, expanding your stomach as air in. At least four minutes to inhale. Inhale the air for two seconds before you gently exhale. Breathe through your mouth. It shouldn't take longer than 4 second for you to let all of the air.

3. This should be done for two seconds or so until you feel comfortable. When you're done, your fast-paced breaths should have stopped.

Reduce anxiety-related behaviors by taking steps that are geared towards countering your fear

In the majority of people, the reaction to flight is a routine after the trigger. At first an introvert who is socially anxious might still attempt to convince himself that he should attend the occasion. As time passes, the individual does not want to go. Each time the thought of going to an event is uncomfortable for him He decides immediately not to attend.

You can alter this habit even if you've been doing it for many years. All you need to do is pinpoint the reason behind your anxiety and then explain precisely the behavior that results from it. You must then determine the gratifying feeling you feel when you decide not to go to an event due to anxiety.

Once you've recognized the cycle of your behavior, it is time to connect negative feelings with the practice. Imagine the negative results from the practice. Write them down to be reminded of the negative impact which the practice has had for you. This will make your mind believe that this habit is not doing anything good for you.

Then, you must come up with a change in behavior as a result of the trigger. In the previous paragraph it is the trigger that triggers first. Then comes the routine of habit. The trigger emotion and anxiety will be present. It is impossible to change it. However, you can alter your behavior in response to the fear. If you're a person who avoids your family's holiday meals because of an embarrassing event. Every time you think about the occasion, you are shamed within. In time, this fear has turned into a fear that the exact incident will occur in the near future.

You must decide whether or not whether or not to take the plunge. You should not be arguing with yourself, or make a decision that isn't the option of whether or not you will go. If you've decided you'll go to the next destination the next obstacle will be thoughts that bring memories of the painful moment. To avoid it from impacting your decision, be looking for an opportunity to alter your habits each time the memories of those experiences pop into your head.

Instead of thinking about it, simply say "I'm planning to" and then think of a different idea. If your anxiety about social gatherings is a problem, use this phrase. The act of saying it can create confidence in many people. It signifies the shift in behavior which will allow them to return to social gatherings for the good.

Then, you need to determine the trigger before it occurs. Each time you experience the fear, you should begin anticipating the reaction that comes after. It is recommended to employ the same phrase as above or any variant of it in order to keep your mind from slipping into habit.

Let your mind be exposed to your fears

One of the most effective methods to overcome anxiety is to confront it head on. It can be overwhelming when you confront all of your fears in one go. Better to take them on by one at a time. Instead of attending all social events you're invited to, concentrate your attention on only one. Once you've been to the event, you need to think about the next one which you'll be attending. It is important to ensure that the worst-case scenario you imagine in your head is your own irrational fear and is likely to never happen.

After attending many social gatherings, you'll be able to begin to enjoy the enjoyment. You'll begin to build confidence in yourself when you're worried regarding an activity. When you attend numerous events, your routine of attending them starts to form. Once this habit has been established, then the magic occurs and your confidence will take an immediate change for the very best. The trick is to change your behavior.

# Chapter 7: The Art of Finding Your Way in Life As an Introvert

How do you find your sweet spot for introverts.

While there is a growing recognition of introverts as well as our specific collection of strengths and positive characteristics, we live in a world where extrovert beliefs dominate. We are told to develop the personal branding of our brand. take the spotlight, lead to be heard, and stand out.

In the world of business open floor plans for offices and lively group discussions as well as brainstorming meetings are how work is completed.

At school, children who are quiet are scolded if their hands aren't raised. They are required to work regularly within large teams.

In social situations In social settings, the "life of the social gathering" are the social butterflies who chat with anyone as well as mix and mingle like their lives was on the line.

Which leaves us those of us who prefer to can do their best on their on our own, but who could find themselves feeling exhausted and overwhelmed in a room filled with strangers?

In my personal life I have spent a lot of time thinking about my introvert nature. Remorse without reflection is an energy waste. Any regrets you may be feeling in to deep reflection as well as constant movement.

Think About Your Gifts

"Gifts" may appear as a heavy word to you. It's a way to describe the distinctive mixture of talents, characteristics, and natural traits that form your personal characteristics. Keep in mind that the term "gift" implies that you don't have to keep them all to yourself . Share your talents and skills with others in order to let them shine.

Let's create an inventory. What are you skilled at? What are you able to contribute to your job? In the course of a relationship? With family and friends?

Here's my list of short-lists:

I'm extremely loyal

I am a lover of listening and assist others

I can predict the thoughts

I am sensitive to other people

I am a committed worker

I am able to focus my attention on the issue and then troubleshoot it

Which items are on the list? Make a list of it. Place your list in a place where you'll be able to easily access it. You should read it frequently. Remember it. This will change your perception of yourself and your place in the world around you.

You are More than an Introvert

This book is focused on making smart decisions to be successful being an introvert and succeed in this world. However, it's essential to understand that even though introversion is a crucial aspect of your character however, it's not the sole aspect that defines you as a person. Are you a soccer player? Artist? An entrepreneur? A stand-up comic? A sensitive person? An intellectual? They all are parts of your personal collection.

Personally, I find great confidence in the fact that I am an introvert. I can recall being a young child at school and feeling a bit discordant with a lot of my peers. When everyone else seemed enjoy the competitive sport as well as working in groups and the noisy playground, I wanted to be part of a small group of my friends taking a quiet moment at the library. I'd like to know that someone told me "It's okay. It's okay to be an introvert. Your preferences and feelings are perfectly natural." What an incredible relief it could have been!

But . . . If being an introvert feels like you're not able to express yourself or feel "locked into" in any way then it's time to shift your attention away from the term. Be aware that introversion exists on an extensive continuum. Be aware you're not in an "either/or" situation. There is no need to pick between being either an introvert or extrovert. All you have to do is be and keep in mind that you have plenty of room for you to explore the range. There are days when you appear more extrovert than other people. This is perfectly normal, and it's healthy. It's not a matter of living in the box. There is more to you than one one thing.

Life Hacks for introverts

In this article, I'd like to give you some actionable techniques that will enable you to navigate the world in a confident manner and make the experience more enjoyable. Let's get started.

Master the art of making Small Talk

Extroverts are adept for creating conversations everywhere they travel. Even if you're not a fan of small talk, it's inevitable. Here's a hint for those of you who are shy: making small talk really isn't so difficult. Here are some tips:

- Keep it simple. Make sure to stick with topics which are uplifting. Talking about small talk should be enjoyable Therefore, it is best to stay clear of topics that are bleak, such as criminality, economic hardship or war.

You can steer the conversation towards an area you are interested in. The reason small talk so difficult for those who are shy is the fact that it may seem too snooty. Small talk can suddenly become more interesting if you speak about something you're fascinated or know about.

Find extroverts. My first thought when I am at a large gathering is to search for people who are also introverts. But, if you are stuck at a party with anyone to talk to you can make small-talk with the people who are extroverts. Extroverts are naturally good at talking and introverts are naturally good listeners. Do you see where I'm getting at here? It's a good fit. The risk is that you get stuck in a monologue. This can be avoided with questions, and be prepared to leave when you feel stuck.

Inspire stories. If you're talking with someone you don't get to have a good relationship with is a fantastic chance to gain new perspectives. Pose open-ended questions that prompt the person to give lengthy responses, and perhaps even tell stories. A great method to meet one another is to ask "What is it that you are doing for an income?" But be sure to follow it by asking "How did you become involved in this field of work?" Getting people to relate their experiences is the most effective way to connect on an even deeper level.

Remember that golden rule: Arrive late, depart early. If you have control over the time you get to and from any type of professional or social occasion, make use of it. Be sure to arrive a little later but not to upset the hosts, or create disruptions naturally. Simply arrive early enough to ensure you can see that your event begun. The goal is to reduce the amount of energy and time you'll have to put into on socializing and not miss out in meeting new people or having fun at the event. If you show up early for an event, it's likely that you'll be exhausted and ready to return home at the end of the night. Be careful not to exhaust your social energy in a hurry.

Make a list of "Personal Rechargers"

I'm going to request you to create a second list. It's an absolute mess. My concern for you is how do you sleep?

What do you do to recharge? What can you do to feel refreshed once more?

Personally, I am feeling reenergized when I:

- Get a great night's rest

I walk my two dogs

• Read a book

• Have a lengthy chat via cellphone with my mother (or another friend who is a good one)

I'm going to enjoy a glass of vino with my partner

- Relax in a bubble bath.

- You can go for an outing on a sunny day.

If you look closely five things on my list are activities I do by myself. Since I'm an introvert, it is my pleasure being alone for long periods of time as it is when I can do my bestthinking, deeply thinking. It's the way I let my mind go and unwind. However, it's not the only way to refresh and relax. However, this is the most important time to my physical, mental and spiritual well-being.

Now, it's your turn. What makes you feel like you're a new person once more? Write it down and keep it near to your heart. When you're overwhelmed return to your list.

## Chapter 8: How Being an Introvert is different from dating An Extrovert

What makes being an introvert different to being an extravert? It certainly is, and in numerous ways. It is important to determine who you are going to meet or plan to meet is an extrovert or an introvert. It is a pretty simple difference to notice almost all the time. Here's the story of how I came to this conclusion in my own single life. I was eating dinner with a few friends when I met an unknown man. I'd never met before. Was it possible to tell from his manner of walking and how he carried himself? It's not possible for me to tell but I thought I should figure it out fast because I was intrigued by him.

My friends request for this man to join our group. Since I'm an introvert and I don't have any acquaintances with him, I may feel a bit uncomfortable. What was I to do? I sat down and watched his behavior and his interactions. Does this person seem to be very active and takes control of the conversation after he has settled down? Are they charming and funny even when he is dominating the conversation, shifting the topic from the one it was prior to his arrival? Does he seem confident and confident? Does he appear impulsive and enthusiastic? These could indicate an extrovert who is sitting next to me.

But, on the other hand is he as quiet and reflective like me? Are they sitting in a secluded spot in awe of the surroundings and people the same way I do? Do you think he understands the "lay of the landscape' before he begins speaking? Does he have more questions about me than focusing on himself? Do you think he's been paying attention when he speaks? All of these are indications of an introvert like me.

It is not necessary to know in advance if you'd rather be with an introvert or an extrovert. However, you must be aware of the indicators so that you can identify what characteristics this attractive person across from you exhibits. Be aware of the responses you give to romantic potential Do you feel more drawn to introverts, or are it the extroverts that speak to you?

Then I discovered that this man was an introvert, and towards the end of the night I decided to meet him for dinner. I'm naturally cautious that If the introvert I'm meeting is too similar to me, it won't be a good fit. We went to the cinema. We had a few conversations during the journey but the silence we had to share was uncomfortable. If we were friends, that the silence between introverts could be filled with emotion and calm. The silence was filled with our anxiety and self-consciousness. I decided not to take him out for the rest of the night. I realized that I required someone to help me balance myself more, and not become an exact copy of myself.

Let's turn this guy into an extrovert, like my current friend. We'll go to the exact film. As we drive to the theater, my extrovert chats at a relaxed pace, and I could just ask him a few questions about himself as we travel through. As we get to the theater, I've got an idea of who is he and as an extrovert, he's been enjoying discussing himself. We'll go for a second date. We'll have the chance for him to meet me in time. It could work out.

It for me , is the main difference from dating an introvert and being with an extrovert. This is in itself an benefit for the introvert. Naturally, you are cautious and you won't jump into. By doing this you'll learn the details about who he really is.

This is crucial details for you to understand what you will do when you be interacting with him.

The First Dates of the Extrovert

While you are on the way to the cinema The extrovert in you begins to share his story with you. He reveals where he works and what he enjoys about his job, how is his favorite social activity and what he believes in politically. In less than an hour, you'll be able to are more familiar with this person than he could have on you in one month. For introverts, spending time with this man would be exhausting. To me, this persona is refreshing and allows me the opportunity to feel familiar with the possible relationship without needing to share too much about myself.

I was not very open about myself, however this just increased his curiosity about me. He thought I was "shy" but the truth is that he wasn't sure for who I really was. I knew a amount about him, but I knew nothing about me. It's true that a lot of what I know about him could be just surface. The majority of extroverts don't reveal more about their personal lives when they first meet unlike introverts. They're just more comfortable in small conversations and small talk makes up an important part of what goes on during the first date.

When you go on an additional date with your introvert , it is essential to take note of all of this. You don't know the guy despite all his talks. It's going to take some time. If you agree to the invite for another date, you're still experiencing the anxiety most introverts feel when they interact with people they don't familiar with, and who is different from them, but one who is significant in their lives.

## Initial Dates With the introvert

As I said earlier the first time I met the introvert was not going well. I found out that the engineer was his name, and that's about everything I knew. He didn't provide any information and I did not even ask. Oh no! Two introverts alone, with nothing to talk about with one another. This isn't the case for any introvert. It just was that we were similar in our degree of introverts. We did not use our most effective skills to meet one another. We did not build any relationship with the other. We did not use their listening abilities to establish a connection with one another.

## Review

In the end, there are some major distinctions between dating as the introvert or an extrovert. The distinctions are evident at the beginning of the process of dating, such as the first meeting and first date. When you meet two people who might or might not be interested in romantically one another The introvert and the extrovert will behave in a different way.

The extrovert who is active and enthusiastic is trying to impress others by using words and stories. For an extrovert, their actions is centered around activity or people. Whatever it is that they are focused on, it will be focused on external factors. Therefore, the person who is extrovert is discussing what they could accomplish or about people they are aware of, as well as the things you can do in a group if you go out with each other. They'll be stimulated by the conversation they share with you. The person who is extrovert needs to realize that the introvert requires some time alone to think about all the input by the extrovert. The person who is extrovert needs to realize that the introvert is receiving an massive amounts of information and it's going to require some time to process all of it. The majority of introverts are confused by this. They aren't sure how to handle this because it's so alien to the way they are living their lives.

The introvert, who is focused in their own space will try to impress others with their stories and stories , and trying to absorb them. It's not that you are shy. You're an introvert. You are taking in everything that your extroverts say and saving it to be able to analyze it when you're on your own. You're able to get into a lengthy, passionate dialogue with the extrovert however, you're not as invested in the result that the discussion will produce as an extrovert is. This is due to the fact that you are at a zen level and are grounded. If you're not talking it's not because aren't interested in dating the person. It is more likely that you are processing your inner thoughts and emotions. Processing is essential to the way that introverts move through life.

After the initial meeting After the meeting, you'll move on to the dating stage. In this stage, the introvert and the extrovert respond differently to the complexities to the relation. It is also based on how the person who is extrovert is grounded externally, whereas the introvert is internal grounded. It is crucial for the extroverts to "share the persona they have and be extremely outspoken and outspoken about the same. For the person who is extrovert, the phrases they communicate to the introverts must be evidence of their dedication and their emotional affluence. The extrovert could make use of a lot of words, but actually communicate only a few. It could be more words than actual substance.

The introvert on the other hand may struggle to express their inner self to the point that the extrovert believes the introvert isn't emotionally accessible. It's only the introvert's reticence which is mistaken for the absence of emotion. Introverts are generally hesitant about sharing their weaknesses since they're not sure how much and what to discuss. They don't feel comfortable speaking about themselves in that way.

To be able for this relationship to go beyond the initial date, both the introvert as well as the extrovert must have an first understanding of why they respond in the way they do. Therefore, don't hesitate to inform the extrovert you're dating to tell them that you're introverted. Ask them to help discover what they value for being an extrovert. Discuss with them what is meant by being an introvert and how you aren't just shy'.

Next chapter we'll talk about what to do and not do in dating an introvert, and establishing a long-term relationship.

## Chapter 9: Begin With You

Individuals have discovered unique ways of discovering their individual strengths and talents. Because of life's changing conditions one can change through a variety of extreme personalities to another. That's why tying yourself to the traits of introversion is not important. You may be able to alter your personality by self-improvement and learning new things.

Your individuality is formed through knowledge, culture and genetics, as well as the impact of your life experiences.

Think about the neuroplasticity of your brain.

The brain has the amazing capability to shape, change, and develop based on its health. It is shaped by different experiences as well as other environmental influences. For instance gray matter is formed in the brain when you acquire an additional language or master a new ability. Traumas that are emotional or physical or modifications in your diet and fitness can affect the state of your brain.

It also means that your emotions, moods confidence, and perception of fear may change. If you're determined enough to change those aspects begin by improving your brain's chemistry with healthy changes to your diet, fitness and active learning.

Here's a step-by step guide to empower yourself to be prepared to create and manage positive and meaningful relationships.

1.) The most important step you should make is to enhance the overall fitness and health of your body. Through consuming a balanced diet consisting of whole food and essential supplements, as well as sufficient physical activity will help maintain the health of your whole brain and body chemical processes. Eat foods, herbs and supplements that offer full nutrition for the body as well as your mind require and stay clear of anything that can cause inflammation or negative results.

If you are able to regulate your brain's chemistry and you'll be able to accelerate your learning abilities and will have greater cognitive understanding. You'll be more open to positive changes that occur that occur in your life, since your brain can recognize the smallest opportunities that could aid in your growth and longevity. Also, you'll experience better control of your mood which increases your ability to cope for your life's challenges. Talk to a medical professional, nutritionist, or fitness instructor for an individualized program of development for you.

2.) Think about therapy or taking medication If you think you might be suffering from the more severe symptoms in social anxiety. Consult an expert in mental health for more information.

3.) Review your environment in terms of social. Take note of the culture and social life which you are constantly by. Think about the types of people that you frequently encounter. Be aware of their attitudes, values plans, goals, motives as well as their motivations, consistency in behaviors, styles of communication as well as conflict management abilities, relationships and initiatives. You are five people who are always present within your life. Their individual qualities and levels of emotional support are transferred to your life in an extremely profound way.

You should surround yourself with those who are in the same boat with you and who will actively support your goals. Look for people with the characteristics you'd like to emulate particularly those who are willing to assist and truly understand your needs. Find support groups, mentors forums, meet-ups, instructors, trainers or the leaders... being around individuals whose characteristics you'd like to adopt can really affect your life over time.

4.) Remove the amount of distractions in your life particularly your normal comfort mechanisms. Many people "escape" to entertainment media such as television, video games radio, and other leisure activities. They can be relaxing however they are not able to fill most of your time. What you do in your spare time can affect your attitude towards relationships. What entertainment you enjoy provides will give you a brief feeling of relaxation however it also causes a change in the perception of reality and your communication style which can affect your interactions with others in real life.

Your time spent with friends will be more significant than the time you're spending on things. Social interactions that are complex can be more difficult and emotionally stressful than playing a gaming console, however with perseverance and patience, as well as a consistent commitment, you can create relationships that are extremely satisfying for an entire lifetime.

5.) Always read. Discover new perspectives on life. Form opinions. If you are more aware of your feelings as well as thoughts on people or things, the more opportunities you'll have to voice your thoughts. The way you read and the content you read, you read it is significant as well. We consume information from sources like magazines, newspapers reading books for leisure, comics, and entertainment websites. It is essential to read only the information that is immediate for your objectives, so you don't become overwhelmed by an overwhelming amount of information. Be very selective about the quality of informationyou read, as well as the amount of information you consume.

Information overload can make you get caught up within your mind. It is easy to become overwhelmed with confusion, disorientation, and confusion. Make it easier to understand the various kinds of information that go through your mind and the factors that shape your view. Being well-read is a method to engage in conversations about everything.

To help you with your learning and memory efforts over time to improve your memory by using the right combination of brain-boosting foods supplements, herbs, and nootropics (also known as neuro-enhancers).

Click here to go to Memory boosters: how You Can Improve Your Memory with Supplements, Nootropics and natural Foods

6.) You can also enhance your conversation skills through practicing mental presence. Being more aware of your emotional state and having more self-awareness can allow you to develop the sensitivity and sensitivity to respond in situations that are unique to your. Meditation and reading along with better mental and physical well-being will improve your self-awareness and your emotional awareness. This balance within can help you stay at the moment, get free of thoughts and generate positive feelings through interactions. Even if it's difficult to know what you should say in the conversation, your great mood, energy , and increased mental alertness will increase your imagination to think of whatever comes to mind.

Social interactions that are varied also give you examples for creating connections. The more you experience the more you will be able to make something meaningful out of any conversation, even ones that begin as surface low-level conversation. You can think about those connections and create your own unique persona. The challenges of life strengthen your character, therefore don't hesitate to challenge your personal boundaries. Don't be worried about embarrassing situations. Everyone started the same way. When you continue to meet new people Your confidence will increase and your ability to handle different situations will get better.

Consider improv classes for an enjoyable method of enhancing your creativity and sensitivity. Improv helps you concentrate, think creatively and improve your sense of humor in the present.

When you begin to harness the positive emotions and energy that you feel within You can pass that positive attitude to the people who you interact with. If people feel positive energy, they will respond to what you're putting out. Whatever you are feeling, others be feeling it.

7) Make a habit of taking action. Making changes to the things you've always had a comfortable relationship with will require a high degree of motivation as well as a

real determination to make changes. The support of an enviable circle of friends will certainly help you.

If motivation and energy are something you are concerned about take a look at what you may be lacking in nutrition. This book for an inventory of deficiencies that can cause lower motivation and energy levels and also the supplements, natural food items and herbs that increase the neurotransmitters that increase energy and drive.

Click here to go to Motivation Boosters: Increase your brain's chemical reactions with natural Foods and supplements that increase the level of motivation

The long-term improvements are made with small increments over time. Being proactive will help keep the procedure consistent and help you reach your goals much quicker. Additionally, you will be able to create and successfully maintain an extensive set of skills, interests, and activities. This will help in improving your character and confidence.

8.) Furthermore, you can alter the wiring of your brain and body subconsciously through mindfulness, Hypnosis or Neuro-Linguistic Programming (NLP) to change any habit or trait you wish to change! The potential for self-mastery and prosperity is unlimited! NLP Meditation, Hypnosis and meditation have proven effective for many committed and open-minded individuals to help them become more outgoing and relaxed, as well as more energized, healthier, and more shrewd.

It is possible to listen to NLP or Hypnosis audio in a relaxed state of mind or before you fall asleep so that your mind will subconsciously recognize the affirmations. You should play them per day for six months for visible changes in your mood, perception or attitude, as well as energy levels and behaviour.

You may also look for the assistance of an NLP Specialist, Hypnotherapist or Healer. There are many audio-related products for your personal listening.

9) Finally, if self-development over the long term is a major concern for you, take a look at The Shyness as well as Social Anxiety Systems for an reconditioning program.

Find abundance within you

These suggestions are in light of the idea that you need to build a positive, abundant and healthy yourself to give back to those around you. Through increasing your physical and mental equilibrium, you can also build an increased emotional threshold for managing more challenging situations and social settings. There is no way to know how many techniques and steps that you can implement are going to be successful until you've had these basic behaviors and practices in place.

## Chapter 10: Develop Into A More Sociable Introvert

"Take an idea. Give that one idea the priority in your whole life. Think of it, think about it, fantasize about it, dwell on the thought. Let your brain, muscles nerves, all the nerves of your body be filled with the idea and leave all other thoughts to the side.

This is the path to success."

-- Swami Vivekananda

It is possible that you haven't been familiar with the term "sociable introvert" because it is quite contradictory. However, you can step away from your normal routine to become more social and outgoing in spite of the widely held and untrue idea that introverts are not social.

To create an ideal attitude, you have to be aware of the traits that you possess as an introvert.

They like less stimulation, whether physical or social.

They're not always shy.

They love being with friends, also - but not many.

They prefer working on their own and stay clear of crowds and bright lights, or the noise.

They process information in different ways.

They like predictability, making plans and routines.

Being an introvert, it is important to first determine what triggers the most stress or anxiety. In the midst of your comfort zone there's a place in which you are not feeling anxious which could actually help you become more productive.

For instance, introverts do extremely well when they start the new job, even though it can be a bit scary for them. The reason is that they are eager to prove themselves, and they will commit more effort, effort and focus to their job. However others who are introverts may be overwhelmed if they fail to have the skills or have the proper training for the job, and this may affect their productivity.

It's not simple to find your ideal anxiety level. You must be observant of yourself and identify where your anxiety can hinder your productivity. Discover your potential so you can conquer your fears.

Here are 10 tips to help you conquer the social insanity and brashness of your life and make you more social:

You must be willing to test yourself.

If you are able to push yourself beyond zones of comfort You will discover that you're offering yourself the chance to explore new areas and do more than you ever thought feasible. However, this doesn't mean that you'll be an extrovert in a matter of minutes. It is also important to be patient and don't push yourself so far that you'll be close to breaking down. If you try to push yourself out too quickly, or too often and you create more stress for you and your family. Start small by one step at a.

Start with a small amount.

As you make progress on small successes, you'll increase your confidence to attempt something new and daring whether it's talking to a larger number of people or exploring new and exciting cuisine.

Be flexible.

Introverts are more prone to planning and taking their precious time to think things over. You don't need to give up everything and become reckless to the point that you are irresponsible. Begin with smaller goals like taking an unplanned vacation or attending a spontaneity-driven celebration. It is also possible to invite a coworker or friend to breakfast with you. You can take your spouse or partner to a casual date. Explore spontaneity in safe settings to reap the benefits and feel more secure in the future.

Join a social club

Try meeting new people regularly and you'll be better at it. It's possible to start with joining Toastmasters. Be aware that growing requires you to step out into your own comfort zone frequently. Toastmasters can help you do this since you'll meet lots of new people. You can also practice speaking to an audience during meetings. Over time, you'll get more comfortable speaking to the crowd, but you'll need to you get used to it.

Be aware that you don't have to go to nightclubs or bars clubs to meet new people.

If you're looking to break from your shell to meet acquaintances, seek out for events in which you meet new people. You could even create your own social environment. For example, you can set up an informal gathering at your house and invite your guests to bring a person to join them. In this way, you'll be in a comfortable social environment and have the chance to chat with people who you've never had the pleasure of meeting.

Meet face-to-face.

There's something to be said for online friendships and relationships, but you must make it the level of a personal relationship. Make it a point to meet offline so that people aren't total strangers even when you interact with them on the internet.

You can sign up for an yoga class or exercise group.

You are able to maintain your introvert personality while having others around you.

Join an author's club.

If there aren't any in your neighborhood, then create one. Reading is among the most cherished activities for people who are introverted. A book club can turn it into an activity that is social. It is possible to connect with new people who share your passion and opinions. Book clubs don't regularly meet, so it's an excellent option for people who are not social to meet and socialize without becoming exhausted.

You can enroll in the acting classes.

Did you realize you Robert De Niro and Emma Watson are introverts? They are nevertheless excellent actors. Learn to portray a completely distinct character in a safe setting and also be able to discover, analyze and play out various behaviors without fear of being assessed. This will allow you to push past your shyness.

Get involved in a group of musicians. group.

When you are part of an ensemble of musicians and you join a group, you not only have fun and gain knowledge but you'll also have the opportunity to meet friends with whom you share a passion for music. There's not a need to be social as the group is focused on the music , but it's a great way to make yourself visible.

There is no proof that only extroverts are ones who excel in socializing. Although they are more active and have a positive attitude towards social interaction, introverts also enjoy connections and become good communicators.

This week, try to practice your social abilities. There is no need to take up the entire time in through the crowd - simply attempt to talk to only one person at a gathering. If you're struggling try to find someone who is a wallflower in the same way and start an exchange by talking to them about yourself. They might be just as introverted as you, and this could be the start of a relationship.

Make yourself up and go out there. There's no harm making the effort as there is no risk and nothing you can lose.

# Chapter 11: What to Start Conversations

The best method for those who are introverts to cope with his anxiety issues is to start talking to strangers. If you want to change your current routine it is your responsibility to be the first to initiate conversations with people.

How do you establish the habit of beginning conversations:

Do not engage in conversation that is tinny and set a clear goal when you are communicating

Introverts aren't a fan of small conversations. If you are talking to people, you need to be able to achieve an end purpose. A clear goal can separate a worthwhile conversation from a casual one. The goal doesn't have to be vital. But, you must be able to provide a reason for engaging in the conversation.

In environments where the objectives are clearer. Sometimes, you must communicate in order to accomplish your task. You might also have to be able to communicate in order to establish relationships with your coworkers or clients. Certain people are proficient in the field of transactional communication. These kinds of communications have the goal of closing a deal and making a sale, and convincing other people to take an action.

However, the goals of communication may extend beyond the realm of professional communication. Your goal in conversation may simply be stop boredom or learn more about the person you are talking to. In the case of meet someone new and you are able to connect with the person, you could determine if you have similar interest through asking them questions.

Keep your goals brief and easy

If you are planning to talk with someone you've never met immediately identify a purpose for the conversation. Do not overthink your goals since it can cause you to be more stressed.

Keep your goal brief and easy to quickly achieve it. Simple goals that are short and concise are simple to remember even when you're engaged in the conversation. When you are suddenly out of ideas to talk about you can always return to your purpose. When you think of your objective when you're in this situation you won't seem like you're talking to yourself to avoid awkward silence.

There is no need to speak to anyone around you

Many introverts feel under pressure when they socialize because they believe that everyone is watching them. They feel they're compared to those who extroverts usually attract most of the spotlight.

If you're in a social situation be sure not to be too concerned about the opinions of others about you. Instead, focus on the people who are interesting in the room and begin speaking with them. Your goal should guide you in deciding whom to speak to.

If the purpose of your social event is to create more connections with potential clients You should speak to those who might be curious about what you're offering.

Create a list of things you are interested in.

The majority of people are unable to find words to speak about because they don't understand the topic being discussed. You can stay clear of these situations by bringing up topics that are interesting to you. If you are a movie buff discuss the latest film you've seen. If you enjoy gardening then discuss gardening as well. If you are aware of areas you are knowledgeable about, you'll feel comfortable in launching conversations.

Note the way you begin conversations with your current group of friends.

Like we said earlier, many introverts have a regular interaction with their circle of acquaintances. This means that they're able to communicate well when they feel at ease with the people they are speaking to.

When you interact with your friends, focus more to the way in which interactions begin or the way it happens. The details involved in the process of communicating can be so insignificant that you tend to overlook the details. It is important to observe interactions and search for specific patterns.

For instance, you can find out who usually starts the conversation. It is also important to observe how you typically begin taking part. You only talk when person asking you questions? Do you initiate interactions with your group of friends?

If you're the initiator and you are the initiator, then you can use your style of communication to other people who are not in your circle. It is easy to start communicating with people who behave as normal. If you know how to begin conversations with others, you don't need to change your appearance in order to be socially accepted.

If you're just a person who is not the initiator You must begin engaging in conversations within your group of friends. This way you can develop your communication skills with those you feel comfortable speaking with. Additionally, you will gain confidence to begin conversations with those outside of your circle. Then, you can take the lessons you've learned when you interact with individuals outside of your circle.

Learn to master the art of asking questions

Being able you can ask questions an essential technique to use when talking to people you have never met before. When you make inquiries, you demonstrate to those you're speaking to that you are keen on their lives. It's an easy way to encourage someone to be more open.

Being able to ask the right questions lets you know the desire of the other person to talk with you. If you ask someone to do something and they provide an extended answer, it indicates that they are ready to speak with you. In the event that the person whom you are talking to is not interested in speaking, they'll inform you of this through what they say in their responses or their response and the non-verbal signals they're sending to you. If you come across an individual who isn't ready to share their thoughts, it is an indication to end the conversation and look for someone else to talk with.

In the ideal scenario you will be able to establish trust with someone by asking questions. Someone who is skilled at asking questions can manage conversations without speaking too frequently. They let other people speak. They're comfortable as the one to listen.

Have a strategy for your exit

Conversations are usually awkward when both parties don't know how to conclude it. You can reduce the awkwardness of lengthy conversations by having an exit plan. There are many methods to accomplish this. It is possible to simply inform the person you're talking to that you've got another meeting to attend. At work you could claim that there is a lot of work to attend to. There are a variety of excuses you can make to get out of a conversation , but it's better to choose a genuine and legitimate excuse instead of lying.

Learn about the most common courtesies of the new class of people

When you interact with a brand unfamiliar group, it is important to be conscious of the informal manner of courtesies that they're practicing. This is especially important when you are interacting with people of people from different cultures. If you think a particular action could be possibly offensive, don't take it. Be cautious when discussing sensitive issues such as religion, politics, and other issues that are important to the people in the group.

## Chapter 12: What's Stopping You from Getting Extroverted?

You are responsible for your own behavior for why you're an introvert. Don't believe that you were born this way currently, and alter yourself to be the person you've always wished to become. The reason that your introverted side is so dominant is because of your mental model of thinking. To help you get an idea about how to keep yourself from becoming an extrovert, here's the mental blocks that were discussed in the earlier chapter.

You undervalue extroversion

If you're an introvert, you might think that you don't require the company of others to lead the life you think of as "normal". There is nothing wrong with being alone but you shouldn't ignore the benefits can be derived from interact with others. In particular, you'll make new friends, you are able to learn new things, which will help you develop as a person. Additionally, you are able to have fun and laugh.

But, it doesn't necessarily mean you must put less importance on being an introvert. It's about finding a equilibrium between the two. You are still able to look forward to time spent alone at home after a long day of socialising You can use the "me period" to read up on what you've been reading or to meditate or even watch one or two episodes of your favorite television series. After you've have had enough time for yourself it's time to meet friends then rinse and repeat.

You are surrounded by the wrong types of people

The reason you are unable to get yourself to be social is due to your social circle isn't the best for enjoying yourself. If you're surrounded by people that you don't necessarily like, it might be the reason you're the way you are today. If you believe that being social is being around the type of people you'd rather not have around, Finding the motivation to meet new people could be difficult.

It's time to get involved in your social circle. Go out and increase your network of acquaintances and friends. Don't be fooled into thinking that you won't meet people you want for a relationship with. They are all around and you only need to grab yourself by the bootstraps and find them.

You think that online socializing suffices for you

In this time when social media has become the norm and you might think that communicating with others online is sufficient for "human" interactions however, it doesn't. Sure, the internet has made it much easier for individuals to stay to know each other as people can communicate with one another even when they're in different parts of the globe. Additionally, they are able to see an insight into what's going on in their lives thanks to social media sites like Facebook as well as Twitter. However, social media can't compare to face-to-face interaction.

When you interact with an individual face to face and face to face, you create a sort of emotional bond between each another. In addition to transmitting information more quickly than typing it out on the keyboard, but you also get non-verbal signals. You can tell if someone else is feeling strongly about his opinion when you hear the excitement in his or her voice as they speak while conversing. On the contrary, you'll be able to determine if the person is opposed to your viewpoint when they use the defensive manner of speaking. It is possible that you can learn all this information through video chats but tone of voice isn't the only non-verbal signals people employ. They also touch one another to make their point clear or make others realize that they are in the same boat.

You don't have any social abilities whatsoever

Are you saying that the reason you don't want to go to parties because you don't know what you'll need to do once you're there. There is no need to fret about it because you can develop the social skills. Socially minded people weren't born like that, their environment and their upbringing shaped them into the people they are today.

Even if you started developing social skills further into your life that doesn't mean you'll never be able to master them. In fact you can show your dog old tricks.

You believe you'll become the type of person who you would rather not be.

There are people who can be quite loud and annoying, however it's wrong to assume to think that you'll be that type of person. If you believe that you'll be the type of person who will talk to someone at a social gathering and then forget the person's name on the next morning then you're not right.

You can be an extrovert you've always wanted be. You can make the choice to be not the annoying kind, but one who is able to engage in conversation with a stranger, and still be truly curious about the things that someone else is talking about. That is you'll be able to avoid becoming someone who enjoys socializing simply for the sake of it.

These are just a few of the mental blocks which hinder you from developing your extroverted side. Examine your own thoughts and determine which of these thoughts is limiting your personal development. There's no reason to not acknowledging any of these negative views, you simply have to acknowledge the fact that they exist and then devote your attention on making sure that you don't contemplate them. It will take some time to adapt to a new method of thinking. And it will certainly be awkward initially, but just maintain a straight face and then move on.

# Chapter 13: Celebrities Introvert Personas

"One of the main motives for men to pursue the sciences and art is to escape from daily life. A well-tempered nature desires to escape the confines of the private daily routine into the realm of objective thought and perception."

--Albert Einstein

FEW OF THE WORLD'S WELL-KNOW INTROVERTS

There is no need to shout to get people pay attention. Many of the most famous and influential people on the planet were introverts. If you believe that you are not able to contribute to the world since you're an introvert, take inspiration from the following individuals who made use of an introvert's strengths, and became successful as a result of it.

## Albert Einstein, Physicist

In some way or another, Einstein always had a struggle at school. The school's headmaster advised his father that he couldn't achieve success in any profession. After moving to Italy and he was unable to do poorly in school and even considered quitting. In the later years of his life, He decided to pursue a career as an electrical engineer. He graduated at a university situated in Zurich, Switzerland, and this was the start of his major contribution to the advancement of science.

The person who developed his theory on relativity frequently described as an introvert. A large portion of Einstein's deep and abstract thinking is surely, derived from his introverted nature.

Albert Einstein is a great role model for those who are shy to showcase their introvert sides. If you can harness your introverted traits You could become the next biggest thing in your field.

Barack Obama, US President

Many believe Obama, the African American who was the first person to be elected as President of the US President, Barack Obama, is an introvert. The way he leads is what causes US citizens be quiet and think for an extended period of time.

Prior to pursuing his career in politics, Obama was a teacher lawyer, civil activist and lawyer. Despite his shy nature Obama was a confident and skilled public speaker. His ability to process the thoughts, problems and opinions of others allowed him to use his exceptional communication skills. His likable personality led to his being admired by the public even more, to the point that they elected him again in 2012.

JK Rowling Writer, JK Rowling

Harry Potter is probably one of the most loved book series ever. Although it's been a while since the Harry Potter Series already ended however, it continues to attract new fans.

The brain behind this enthralling novel can be traced to the legendary JK Rowling. She has said it was her idea to come up with the idea while on a trip across the country from Manchester from Manchester to London. Her website states, "I simply sat and was thinking for about four hours as all the details exploded in my head and this scrawny bespectacled, black-haired boy who was unaware that it was a wizard began to become ever more apparent for me."

Her brilliant writings also contributed to the popularity of novels. A few of them are Stephanie Meyer's "The Twilight Saga,""

Suzanne Collin's "The Hunger Games,"" and the novel by Veronica Roth "Divergent." They are novels are influential, not just for readers, but for ordinary people too.

Introverts such as JK Rowling did not just believe in what they could accomplish. They were enthralled by their journeys of learning. Each has their unique style of telling stories and it has won the hearts of many across the globe.

Bill Gates, Microsoft co-founder and chairman

Before computers were accessible to everyone, Bill Gates already spent endless hours playing with them. His deep interest in computers led him to develop Microsoft and create the highly well-known Windows Operating System. Today, the majority of computer systems in the world operate on Windows. While there are other operating systems to choose from but many users still opt for Windows due to its flexibility and simplicity of use.

Thanks to his achievements through Microsoft, Bill Gates is now among the richest people in the world. He didn't let his literary and quiet personality stop him from following his dreams and ideas; instead, utilized them to benefit himself.

Mark Zuckerburg, Facebook founder

Facebook is the biggest and most well-known social media platform in the world. Nearly everyone on the planet is using it. Today, Facebook is more than an instrument to stay connected with relatives and friends. It's also a place for advertising, memories, entertainment , and self-expression. If it weren't for Facebook's founder, Mark Zuckerburg's introversion Facebook would not be the place it is today. it is now.

## Allison Harvard, Top Model

It's not possible to be a enthusiast of America's Next Top Model if you do not know Allison Harvard. Though she didn't take home the title America's Next Top Model in both seasons she was a part of, Allison is one of its most famous contestants. Who has forgotten those large round and blue doll eyes? Who doesn't have a chance to recall her strange fascination with cat blood?

Allison is not just strange in appearance, but she also acts this way. Although she is able to remain quiet in one spot while the ladies are enjoying themselves, Allison is unable to avoid the attention of the viewers of the show. Because she's not ashamed of her unique quirky. That's exactly what people love about her.

Hayley Williams, Musician

Paramore's self-titled album has received many criticisms from both musicians and fans. Some believe that it's not the type of music that Paramore is well-known for and others think it to be the most unique of the albums they've released. Although they've evolved in a different way from the way they performed prior to the release, Hayley's choice of words to compose lyrics is a reflection of the original Paramore brand.

However, even if Hayley Williams is an energetic, wild emotional singer She's always been a shy person offstage. She's a woman who's always interested in exploring the secrets of life. It's evident in her blog posts and posts on social media. You can see it in every shift and rise of her voice in her songs.

Her abstract thinking and creativity allows her to go beyond what is basic to philosophical. This could be the reason that many people consider her to be the Illuminati. However, like many introverted musicians her music simply is a reflection of her interest in the inner world.

Taya Smith Worship Leader

Taya Smith is currently one of the worship leaders of Hillsong United. Christian group, Hillsong United. For a long time, Hillsong has been the most loved group for creating incredible worship songs. Their music has served as the primary song of faith of many people throughout the globe. If you've ever seen Taya Smith's voice, you know what they've been feeling.

Nobody can tell the extent to which an introverted Taya Smith is in real life However, there's one thing for certain. Taya's quiet nature hasn't prevented her from being a living for something she absolutely loves sing for God. This humble act of worship changed thousands thousands of individuals. It sparked illumination for those who were lost in darkness. It gave hope and comfort for those who were in fear.

From the Heart

Similar to the others, you can accomplish amazing things. You don't have to be visible for people to be noticed by others. All you require is an inner heart that is never stopped thinking and a mind that doesn't stop thinking.

Perhaps introversion is not well-known even within Einstein's time and that's the reason he failed at school. However, as he grew older maybe he understood that the difference didn't matter.

It's fine to be still. There's nothing wrong with having weird thoughts. It's fine being different. It's not going make you less human. In fact it can make you feel more alive than before.

It requires lots of stares at nothingness in order to make a great story or a tune. A lot of thinking is needed for the creation of creative concepts like Facebook as well as Windows OS. The ability to think clearly is crucial to guide the fifty countries of America. It takes many quiet moments to stop for one moment and think, "What can I do for the world?"

# Chapter 14: Maximizing Introversion

There are plenty of introverts who always feel like they're out of place anywhere they go, especially in public spaces, at work and even in groups. It's always about who talks more or who gets the most laughter. This can be an issue because they are constantly speaking to people and getting to know people on a humorous basis isn't their strong point. In many cases, prior to being involved in an informal discussion group or meeting, they've been portrayed as the "loner" silent or shy person. The social stigma makes it harder for anyone who is seeking solitude to be an efficient member of the group , let even climb the ladder of professional success. It is becoming apparent to those who are seeking success that success is geared to those who are able to effectively draw attention and apply a novel concept. Keep your cool it is likely that things will continue to shift.

Since introverts are becoming conscious of the favored characteristics of extraverts. They are becoming aware that being introverted does not at all a disadvantage. It's actually an extremely efficient tool, and untapped resource only the taciturns are able to access, an advantage for introverts. The workplace is where the majority of members of society spends the bulk of their time. There is no reason to believe that those who are hesitant can't take advantage of the opportunity by using their own unique talents to make the most of their advantages.

Overcome Shyness

The taciturns may not shy away from talking with people outside of their own circle, but it's not uncommon to observe shyness in a few. If you're shy, and overcoming this is a problem they have to confront first. In contrast to the rest of us introverts don't like being in the midst of other people and are hoping for them to gain knowledge through the process of survival. They do not react very well when "motivated" by violence or threats. For the timid it is a type of attack, and another reason why they lose their energy. The best method to overcome shyness is to let introverts to be aware of the issue. Why and why not need to be addressed.

Why should you talk? Because you've got an idea. Actually, they're more effective ideas that will aid the objectives of the business without taking a lot of risks. It is not your intention to be placed on the same pedestal for your ideas, but you desire to be a productive element of the workforce and to be recognized for the work you have done. Have you ever been in an instance where you were unable to communicate your ideas, and the body that was in charge chose an idea that was more shady than what you had come up with? Do the phrases "My idea was superior" seem familiar? The problem is that not only was this a wrong idea implemented, but the unsound concept and risk came back with a devastating impact on other people's work, including yours. This is a chaotic and noisy environment which can be very stimulating for people who are shy. If you don't want to be a public speaker for recognition, then speak up for the purpose of lessening the noise that impedes your focus and peace.

Talking to strangers is a fear for those who are afraid of conversations because they can be a casual conversation which can veer between topics. Chats are small conversations. Small conversations can change their direction quickly to almost everything. Everyone is expected to keep up with the conversation and participate on various topics. People who aren't naturally inclined cannot navigate this process with ease. They do not just require time to consider what they want to say, but they are also extremely secluded from news and gossip "news" as well as gossips from the workplace. However, communicating with others is the main reason for shyness.

Talk about work. Engage in a one-on one conversation with a coworker at the office. The way you set the scene is important since it informs them that the conversation is focused on what you're working on and how they can assist. The conversation about your job can be beneficial for you being an introvert, you will already know what your job was all about and any queries related to it, you could answer quickly. It also minimizes the possibility of small conversations. This will enable you to manage the flow of conversation unlike group meetings in which the flow could be triggered from any direction and leave you feeling in a state of confusion. This sense of control that you must keep in mind.

You might be wondering about how you can manage speaking in the presence of the crowd. Don't be afraid. Just remember the feeling of control you gained from your one-on-one conversations. It might surprise you to find out that one-on-1 conversations are among the most difficult for those who tend to be introverted. Comparatively speaking in public is a breeze through the park. You might ask why. It's the control of the flow. If you're speaking you decide the pace of your conversation. You can speak slowly and no one will be able to interrupt you or begin throwing your small talk at you. While you're speaking about something you're an expert in people can ask questions and you'll know the answer within your mind. Your domain is yours and they're simply bystanders. It's an advantage for introverts.

Continue to Do What Works

Success for introverts is contingent on the way they use their natural abilities to achieve. It's no secret that introverts gain more through observation, can discern with no disturbance, and are effective in solitude. They are at their best when they're free of the constant noise of the workplace. While others are content with only looking at only at the surface of the concept, slow-witted ones dig deeper and continue to work on it. This is a benefit that employers are willing to invest in to make sure they maximize it.

Steve Wozniak is probably the greatest advocate for working in solitude and in a group. In his small cubicle at Hewlett Packard, he created the Apple computer, which is the first computer to pioneer technological innovation. In the meantime, he's insisting that innovation is not often accomplished in a group. He is right on the money. Solitude isn't only a place for those who are taciturn. It's a method that shields you from the clamorous world. It creates an atmosphere to allow the mind functions. In a quiet environment it is impossible to disturb their thinking process, and they are more productive.

You can work on your own. Continue to do that. Being an introvert, there could be many thoughts in your head that need to be communicated in a way that others can comprehend. Interruptions and disruptions do not help the process of thinking to flow, so they should be avoided. Solitude is a great pursuit for an introvert, and in the big picture of it all the time, when you work at it, you're having fun. It's these small moments that can help an introvert succeed. It doesn't mean groupwork is not a good idea. Research has shown that more effective work has been achieved compared to that which can be accomplished by the group effort. It is more than a plea for employees to take a break in their own private areas when they require. Solitude can be the catalyst to a great performance.

There's no reason to tell you to concentrate on one task at a time since you've likely been doing it for years. Keep doing it. This shouldn't be interpreted to be slow, but rather diligent. It is best to break the work into smaller sections, work through and learn about each and then come up with solutions. Choose which solution is the best one by looking at the potential risks and benefits. This is the best method to understand the task that you are given so that at any time, you will be able to stand your ground and not be astonished by the questions. Every decent employer will value the quality of work over the quantity of their employees' work at any time.

Learn as much as possible as you do. It should be easy since one of introverts' favorite activities is reading. Keep doing it. Always learning is an aspect of the introverts ' world. It's not only thrilling for many, but it's also an essential tool to the ability to achieve success. It is impossible to have any idea what one piece of information could be beneficial for regardless of how basic it seems. However, when you need it you'll be prepared and equipped. The world of introverts could be the perfect location to learn and be ready for any situation.

## Exude Leadership Material

It's not difficult for someone who is introverted to become effective as a leader. Actually the most influential and successful leaders are, in a way, introverted. Think of Abraham Lincoln and Rosa Parks. What can you do to help yourself achieve the status of one?

As a senior employee others will be watching to see if you'd like to or not. This is a chance to demonstrate your subtle yet effective leadership abilities. Be attentive to your employees when they respond to questions and stay clear of interruptions, just as you would like it to be in a conversation. Listening is essential to good management and employees will respond positively when they are taught to listen.

Be aware of your preference for high-quality conversations over volume. Set up one-on-one meetings frequently. These intimate sessions will allow you to focus on particular employee and get better informed about their abilities. This is also the most effective way to increase confidence and avoid making others who are introverted feel exiled.

Introverts' leader is supportive of the initiative and creativity of employees. In giving them the space to think up innovative ideas, they perform better since they determine the pace by themselves. Let them run with their ideas and acknowledge their desire for privacy when they require it. Contrary to introverts Extraverts tend to be intimidated by the insanity of subordinates.

You must make the most of your writing abilities. Bring this skill to your work. Perhaps it's through your office memos. For a greater public, write well-written articles for the magazine that is geared towards industry. There is also the more efficient option of using social media platforms to get your message to the masses. The most appealing thing is that you don't have to speak and can do this from is done from the comfort of your own home.

Recharge

It speaks for it self. Even if you are efficient and effective as a manager, there'll be times when you'll long for solitude. Don't resist this urge or consider it an obstacle or vulnerability. Solitude is the air that sustains you. Without it, there's no doubt that you'll become unproductive at your job. Keep in mind that time alone can also be the source of your epiphany. Make the most of it.

"Did you exhaust yourself just thinking about that?" It was Bessie.

"Yes."

"Did it help your feel more relaxed?"

"A small amount", yes."

"If it is bothering you so deeply, why don't simply apologize?"

"Because I'd need to speak to him once more. Wouldn't it be a bit inconvenient except for work?"

"Maybe. However, you're rude and unfriendly. Everyone should be nice enough to accept apologies."

The word is difficult. She is not a fan of the word "shy. Much more than she dislikes"shy" "shy".

"Fine."

## Chapter 15: Surviving a Full House

Introverts can find it difficult to cope in a bustling home whether it's with family members or roommates who are bouncing around constantly. It can be difficult to get their time alone and it will be even more difficult to maintain a positive attitude due to being pushed into social settings that they're not experienced with or like. In this chapter , you'll learn some strategies to the mind and body in check during periods of stress and increasing social interactions at home.

Although introverts can enjoy long-term visits from family and friends, many introverts can attest to the fact that constant noise and social stimulation can be extremely draining. No matter how much an introverts may feel about their loved ones and family they can get overwhelmed and put the mood or mental health of the introvert in danger. Here are some suggestions to keep sane:

Leave the House

It is essential to get out of your home every once in a while. It is possible to need to leave the home to take an hour for yourself. It's perfectly fine to go out and do it. Take a break for an easy walk, or perhaps volunteer to run things like buying something at the market or drop off any mail that needs to be delivered. Some people who do not have the traits you are able to share this with you since they don't realize that you require time for yourself. Be aware when you reply and remember to stick to your boundaries! Simply explain that you're in need of some time for yourself. Be assured to express your gratitude for the opportunity.

You will wake up earlier than everyone Others

Awaking earlier will provide a new world for you. If you're in need of space to yourself without the distraction of people stumbling around on your back or in your ear, rise earlier than other people! Although getting up earlier could be a little difficult initially, depending on your routine is but it can provide you with some time that you may not have prior to. Even an hour of peace in the early morning hours prior to the time that sun (or any other person!) awakes can be an excellent way to start the day!

Use Headphones

If the home is crowded, it can be difficult to get some tranquility. By using headphones, you can completely block out all the background noise and will make you feel more to being alone than with headphones. You'll be able be able to block out the external noise and be able to go back into your personal space for some time. Be aware of the people who are around you. Don't ignore people who are trying to explain something however, ensure that you are given the time that you require.

Be sure to be flexible

It is important to be flexible, particularly when you're spending time with your family members. Although meeting our needs can keep us functioning at our best, there are moments, we might require putting our needs aside. There could be parties for holidays , or other important social occasions such as birthday parties It is the best thing for you when it comes to maintaining relations with your loved ones to ensure that you attend these occasions.

Here's a list of ways you can engage in a large house to feel like you are being alone:

• Schedule some time for reading your book of choice.

* Take an effort to sit down and read favourite magazine.

* Play games on the computer or a video game.

* Have a hot, long tub or shower.

* Take a walk for a stroll through the neighborhood.

You can listen to music as you work with headphones.

* Work out in your bedroom.

* Draw, paint, or sketch using music.

* Watch a film, (people cannot and should not talk a lot during a film).

* Use the bathroom for 15 minutes. Nobody will be able to bother you while you're sitting on the toilet!

Your spouse may not comprehend your needs because you are an extrovert. It could be beneficial to give them this book to help them to comprehend you better. You'll need to sit down and talk about what you require to do in order to become a full person in your household. It can be a challenging discussion to hold in the event that they're used to pleasing your family members. You may get their emotions wounded, but you must to be completely transparent and truthful and provide information in a way they can comprehend.

# Chapter 16: Reveals. Myths and Misconceptions

"Whatever type of introvert you are, certain people might find you to be "too much" in some ways, and not enough in other ways." Laurie Helgoe

There are lots of misconceptions about introverts.

They may appear to be and lonely often feel lonely, unfriendly, shy or insecure. However, in many cases introverts can actually be an advantage. People who are introverts get their energy from being in solitude, it's like a battery which they recharge which allows them to be out in the world and be able to connect beautifully with others. They take longer to take in information than extroverts and this is because they think more deeply than those who do not, they require more time to process concepts before moving on to new ideas.

We are constantly overwhelmed by messages that tell us you must speak up and stand out to succeed introverts can succeed even more by focusing on their own strengths. Many people think that introverts aren't big but they're actually part of an entire universe in their minds. They are known to say the most in the smallest quantity of words. When they are talking about word economy, introverts are the most efficient economists. They might not be as vocal however they communicate often through their actions. Their silence can be more persuasive than those with the highest level of talk in the room, yet it's important. It is recommended that if you don't have any valuable information to share, it's best to remain silent and let people think you're a fool rather than stand up and show them wrong. I believe that innovation is best when it is in a quiet space which is free from external influences that try to hinder our creativity. I believe that solitude is the key to invention When one is alone, it is when the ideas take root and are able to come forth effectively. Here are some advantages that an introvert can enjoy: they're excellent listeners. They have a natural ability in actively listening. They are the person contacts to vent their frustration or when they have great news to impart; introverts can listen and join them without turning around. Extroverts tend to engage in a conversation before fully digesting what the other person stated. This is not because they're selfish or lack of concern however, they are able to process information in a way that is interactive. I am concerned by our culture, where being single is seen as suspect or unprofessional; and one must be apologetic for it, excuse it and hide the fact that they do it as a secret pastime.

It doesn't require an extrovert in order to influence the world. Neither do you have to be an autocrat to accomplish this. If it's done with a soft touch that shakes all the earth with your thoughts. Introverts are able to process information internally. This ability allows them to listen, comprehend and offer thoughtful insight when they are asked to respond. They consider their words before speaking since introverts are generally less at ease speaking, whereas they are more comfortable listening. They choose their words carefully, and they only speak when they are able to speak, which means there's more chance of having an impact when we speak. However introverts can spend a bit too long to form their thoughts prior to speaking them out, especially in business settings that are fast-paced. The ability to choose words carefully is equally important online as in person, which is why deciding the right words to use in an email is vital too.

They are also observant. In addition to their exceptional listening abilities, introverts have what I call an "superpower" in their ability to observe. We can spot things that other people might not be able to see due to the fact that they are speaking and processing their thoughts out loud. Even though it appears as if they're sitting in a quiet place in a conference in reality, introverts are taking in the knowledge being shared and are thinking about the information. An introvert is also using their ability to be observant to see the environment and the people. They are more likely to observe their facial and body expressions as well as the bodies of people around them, which makes them more adept at inter-personal communication. Introverts are similar to a clean and well-maintained website that takes time to load. There is plenty of exciting things, but most users don't wish to be waiting for to see them open while the extroverts just popping up

ads, they will pop up and attempt to engage even if you're not at all interested.

Introverts are particularly adept at spotting introvert characteristics in other people, they are able to detect when a person is thinking, processing or watching, and allow them to think, process and observe. This helps people feel more relaxed, and they give time to truly be with others. They form lasting friendships because introverts feel their energy draining from being around others rather than extroverts who get energy from socializing with other people. Introverts select their friends carefully They prefer having some close, trustworthy friendships that they can put their energy and time in as opposed to an entire network of acquaintances. Introverts are very selective regarding who they invite to their lives. It is a bit of a commitment to make sure that someone is enter their circle, it's quite a lot. The introvert's personality makes them be attentive, loyal and loyal friends.

They make wonderful romantic partners introverts need their own space to reflect and recharge They can also sense the need for space in their relationships as well. Because we all have a need for our privacy, we also give it to our loved ones too so we don't become emotional or high-maintenance in our relationships. The same traits that make introverts excellent listeners make them excellent partners. After an exhausting day, they're at hand to

listen and encourage their partner ,
without being compelled to speak about
themselves. They allow their loved ones to
be angry and let them vent their emotions
, even if they're not concerned about
making them angry Introverts are known
to apologize, even when they've not done
something wrong, simply because they
value others more than they do their own.

Introverts are also drawn to getting
acquainted before sharing personal details
with a potential partner. This can help
them appear more attractive when they
are in the beginning phases of
relationships. There is something
appealing about the mysterious aspect of
introverts. It can make people curious and
want to get to know the person better.

Introverts are savvy networkers and being
part of a group with the aim to talk, meet
and create a positive impression. This can

be daunting for many, particularly for introverts. However, they can make use of their unique strengths to build lasting connections. The more extrovert of us may attend social gatherings with the intention of chatting with as many people as they can However, often the conversations aren't able to create lasting impressions. However, the strength of networking doesn't always come from the number of people you meet. People who are introverts should concentrate on learning more about the people whom they meet, even if only have contact with a small number of people. People who are introverts strive to make meaningful connections with just a handful of people who they can follow up with in a certain wayafter the event they can send hyperlinks to speeches or articles which made them consider the people they talked to. This kind of active listening and follow-up could be more effective than passing out business cards in a jumble, as I'm sure.

People who are introverts can be great leaders when they harness their strengths naturally. They aren't compelled to be the center of attention and claim all the responsibility for the team's success. Instead they prefer to draw attention to what they can do to help their team. A leader who is extroverted may be visible however, you might notice the leader before the entire team. People who feel appreciated tend to be more enthusiastic. Because introverts are slower to process information and with greater concentration than their extroverted counterparts, introverted leaders are more likely to know more about their subordinates. They hold focused conversations with colleagues to understand their strengths and talents, as well as passions and strengths. Once they've gathered all the information they need, they can make use of what they've learned in order to assist each member of the team to be more productive and more happy working.

When I first started using these dating sites I came across one girl who was an ideal match. It was through her that I started to write. This was my first experience I talked to a person continuously on the phone for hours. I enjoyed having conversations with her, however after a while we realized that we weren't designed for the same person, however, we're still in contact and are good friends today. At times, we check in on messages to find out what's going on in the other people's lives and how the world treating them.

I'd be the one who can solve the riddles and questions in the class first , but would not say a word until you ask me about it. The best way to deal with the introverts is to let them know that you are looking for an inclusive community where they feel like they are belonging and see themselves as part of the community. Don't try to force them out of their group It is possible that they will be an isolated person, but it becomes their routine and they'll start to hate social interactions gradually and slowly.

It's a myth that every person is born with the personality they have, but the truth is that we learn it from people in our lives, our family friends, and particularly our parents. A child's character and mind are as water. Place it in a jug , and it will transform into an ice jug. Put it into a bottle and it will transform into an actual bottle; when you put it in a bowl and it becomes the bowl.

The most cruel way to treat a child is to do so with anger and feelings of inferiority. If the child is not able to be a fan of their parents' company, there is a higher chance that they'll be introverts. If you continue beating or scolding them, the child will be an introvert and might end up becoming an introvert as they reach adulthood. If you let your kids feel like they are inferior to other people and demand too much of them, until they feel pressured that is sure influence how they see the world and how their attitude towards society. which is why another introvert may emerge.

# Chapter 17: Learning To Socialize As An Introvert

The interesting thing regarding learning, is the fact that it's an "never stop" journey. Learning is never-ending. The process of learning begins through childhood until adulthood. Even when one is old is still on the learning process. Being an introvert will not hinder the learning processes. It is essential to grow as a person. To improve yourself you must master how to socialize. As it isn't in at all simple but you can follow the steps each step by taking lessons from other people just as every other child.

Let's consider one child as an illustration. Children learn slowly but continues to learn. In the beginning, he or begins to crawl. After a few months of crawling children learn to stand by his or her mother's. Then, he or starts walking by taking one step at a time, slowly. Then, he examines how people walk, and begins to walk as they do, but faster. Soon, he or she learns how to speak. So, every stage of learning that a child goes through is influenced by the people who are around them. The growth of a child continues to grow, for learning is a endless ocean.

Being an introvert, why don't you try the techniques used by children? Since a child can't take on all the tasks at once but rather, they learn at a snail's speed. Being someone who is introverted, why wouldn't you conceal the traits you have for while and then begin to study other people? Of course you can. As an infant the only thing you need to do is take the steps listed below each step by step.

Make yourself perform that thing that you don't like to do

Thinking about whether you should be the first to extend the hand of greeting your business acquaintance or not? Are you contemplating inviting someone "not not so close" person close to you at your home to spend time with you? Go ahead! It could be difficult at first, but attempt to do it at least once and you'll discover it more easy the next time. You can walk up to your business associate and extend your arms in greeting. Invite your friend from afar to your home for lunch. You'll be able to benefit from these gestures. A business associate who has avoided you in the past is the very first person to meet you on the next day. Your distant friend, who has enjoyed lunch with you is also likely to show appreciation. In this way, the relationship grows stronger over time. Do you remember the trick? You just have to make yourself do it. Are you getting it? Yes! We'll move on.

Get to know New People Every Day

If meeting every day new people will seem like a lot of work Try to get in touch with more than one every day. When you meet new people throughout the course of the days, you will have added many names to the people you've met in the end of the month. Someone you've invited for dinner is likely to be happy for you to meet their other acquaintances. This means that you will encounter new acquaintances, though it is not necessary to develop a long-term connection with them.

Try to lend a helping Hand to Others

Even though you might not be able to assist people all the time, when you havethe ability, let those who are around you know that you're concerned. If you do you have, let your friends know that you are. The people who live near you think of you as an philanthropist, if you're the type of person who is wealthy. This way, you'll be loved by people around you. If there is a program held by any neighbor, this neighbors will be encouraged to invite you to. In return you'll get to interact with other people, becoming more attracted to other people and engaged in more social events. A shy person who is always willingness to lend people the helping hand is forced to connect to them without or her knowledge.

Enjoy your Family members at your leisure Time

Do not waste all of your time on your own. Visit your family members often, and engage with them. If you're the one who comes from an extended family connect more closely with others in your family. Don't restrict your connection to your siblings and parents by yourself. Expand your relationship beyond your parents' home. Explore beautiful places with them. Invite them to accompany you to places they believe you should be aware of. For example, ask that a distant relative to go out with you and rather than your closest family members. They will be delighted to join you especially if he/ they know you are an introvert. In this way, you'll become more social as an introvert.

## Conclusion

In the present there are many people who feel pressured to follow the "accepted" way according to social norms out of fear of being seen as socially excluded. But the truth is that we all are required, whether extroverts or introverts. We all have a place on planet. The best thing to do is not try to appear like the person they aren't, instead, embrace the strengths that they already possess.

I hope this book given you the courage to continue to explore your possibilities and be comfortable in all your activities. I wish you all the best for your networking and business projects.